# About this Book

How many of us know why a religion develops? Do we know why the story of Jesus and his teachings has grown into Christianity, the largest religion in the world?

*Christians and Christianity* traces the growth of the religion from the simple story of Jesus; his actions, his teachings and his death. We read about the first Christians, persecuted for their beliefs; and of the great power the Christian Church held when it became the official religion of the Roman empire. Later many Christians broke away forming different Protestant Churches, and we read how the religion, in its various forms, spread throughout the world.

Christianity has had a turbulent history, deeply interwoven with the growth of European civilization. In the following pages Leonard Hobley tells the exciting, sometimes tragic and often hopeful story of the religion, and shows how Christian thinking governs the actions of most of us today.

# Beliefs and Believers

by Leonard F. Hobley

JEWS AND JUDAISM
CHRISTIANS AND CHRISTIANITY
MOSLEMS AND ISLAM


BUDDHISTS AND BUDDHISM   Martha Patrick
HINDUS AND HINDUISM   Partha and Swasti Mitter
SIKHS AND SIKHISM   S. S. Kapoor

# CHRISTIANS AND CHRISTIANITY

## Leonard F. Hobley

First published in 1979 by
Wayland Publishers Ltd
49 Lansdowne Place, Hove
East Sussex, BN3 1HF, England
Second Impression 1980
Third impression 1982
Fourth impression 1983

Copyright © 1979 by Wayland Publishers Ltd

ISBN 0 85340 719 3

Printed and bound in Great Britain
at The Pitman Press, Bath

# Contents

# 1 Who are the Christians?

Who are the Christians? Why does Christianity have more believers than other religions? Can anyone be a Christian? Can a Christian be recognised by his appearance? Or his language? Or by anything else?

Christianity arose from the Jewish religion. Jesus, the founder of Christianity, was a Jew who had been brought up as a member of an intensely religious nation believing they were God's 'Chosen People'.

Jesus lived at a time when ideas about God were changing. In early books of the Bible God is spoken of as jealous and blood-thirsty. Most Jews accepted this idea, but some of their prophets, such as Isaiah, described God as kind and merciful. This view of God was expressed by Jesus.

Although the Jews believed that God especially cared for them, they had been for centuries a conquered and despised nation. They thought they were being punished for past sins, and longed for a Messiah, a leader who would be sent by God to deliver them from their sufferings. Some hoped for a great king like David, who had ruled them many years before.

So when Jesus, humbly born to a carpenter and his wife, proclaimed himself as the Messiah, most Jews would not accept him. When he taught that God made no distinction between nations, that there were no 'Chosen People', the Jews did not believe him, and rejected him. Paul, the great Christian missionary, travelled outside the borders of Palestine (the country of the Jews) and told the story of Jesus and his life and teachings to the Gentile nations.

The birth of a son to a poor carpenter in the little conquered Jewish nation hardly seemed an

*Schoolchildren leaving church in Roman Catholic Portugal*

event of earth-shaking importance, but that baby, born in a stable, was to change the world far more radically than the mightiest Roman emperor. From the life and teachings of Jesus grew Christianity, which today has more believers throughout the world than any other religion.

There are Christians among all races, living in many countries, speaking different languages. We cannot therefore recognise a Christian by his appearance, his dress, or his language. His religious beliefs may vary too, for there are many different forms of Christianity.

---

*Holy Communion in a Methodist primary school in Rhodesia*

# 2 Birth of Jesus

We know little about the first thirty years of the life of Jesus. He probably lived quietly with his family in the village of Nazareth, with his mother Mary and Joseph the carpenter. He learned the laws and customs of the Jewish religion, and the scriptures of the Old Testament. The record of his life and teachings and the actions and writings of his followers, make up the books of the New Testament.

At that time people's ideas about religion and life were very different from ours. Little was known about science and the laws

*The shepherds worshipping the baby Jesus, born in a stable*

of nature. People thought that God sent natural disasters as punishments for their wickedness. They thought illness was caused by evil spirits entering into people, and that some men had the power to cast out these spirits. They believed comets and stars were signs of important happenings on earth.

People explained things they could not understand by inventing stories about them. This happened with most religions in their early stages, and with Christianity too, stories were told about miraculous events at the time of the birth of Jesus.

The first four books of the New Testament, the Gospels, tell about Jesus's adult life, but they were written many years after his death. The Gospels of St Matthew and St Luke tell of the miraculous birth of Jesus to his virgin mother Mary, after an angel told her that her son was holy, and would be called the Son of God. Matthew tells of wise men from the East following a star which led them to a stable where the baby Jesus lay in a manger. Luke writes of an angel appearing to some shepherds, saying, "Glory to God in the highest, and on earth peace and goodwill toward men. Unto you is born this day in the city of David, a Saviour which is Christ the Lord." Wondering, the shepherds hurried to honour the baby Jesus.

*Jesus helping Joseph the carpenter, with Mary beside him*

# 3  Teaching of Jesus

The Gospels record that when Jesus was about thirty years old, he felt unhappy about the way many priests carried out the teachings of the Jewish religion.

As no records of the actions and sayings of Jesus were made at the time, we cannot be sure that the accounts in the New Testament are accurate, but there can be no doubt about his thoughts, or the sort of person he was. He wandered about the countryside telling people his "Good News". He became known and loved by the common people, among whom he lived, gladly accepting their food and shelter. He was not afraid to talk with criminals and outcasts. When criticized for this, he said that these were the people who most needed his friendship and help.

*Jesus and his disciples on the Lake of Galilee*

He had a wonderful influence over others, and many sick people were healed by his touch. Crowds followed him, and he chose a group of twelve disciples (followers) who went with him, helping with his work of preaching and healing the sick.

Jesus did not begin preaching without deep thought. He went alone to the hills to think and to pray for guidance. He knew that only Judaism, among all the many religions in the Roman Empire, taught that there was one God, Creator of the universe. Jesus was especially influenced by the Jewish prophets, Isaiah, Amos and Jeremiah. Like them, he felt that true religion was a matter of Man's personal relationship with God and of his love and goodwill to other men.

Jesus taught that God is the father of everyone, all men are brothers, and should treat one another as members of one great family, so bringing peace and happiness to the world. He continually taught that men and women should love one another. He said to the people: ''Love your enemies, do good to those who hate you, bless those who curse you and pray for those who ill-treat you.''

He explained his ideas in parables (stories) so that his followers could more easily understand, thus: ''So then, anyone who hears these words of mine and obeys them is like a wise man who built his house on rock. The rain poured down, the rivers overflowed, and the wind blew hard against that house. But it did not fall, because it was built on rock. But anyone who hears these words of mine and does not obey them is like a foolish man who built his house on sand. The rain poured down, the rivers overflowed, the wind blew hard against that house, and it fell. And what a terrible fall that was!''

It is not easy to live as Jesus taught, but he set the example, helping people, healing the sick and comforting the distressed. When he was cruelly put to death by crucifixion, he asked God to forgive those who were crucifying him.

*Jesus teaching in Jerusalem*

# 4  Crucifixion and Resurrection

Jesus's life reached its climax when he entered Jerusalem, where he spoke to the crowds celebrating Passover, the Jewish festival commemorating the Israelites' escape from Egypt. He warned about the false teaching of priests and rulers. He overturned the tables of the money-changers at the temple, where money was being collected by cheating the people. He taught that all men were brothers, and that God had sent him not only to Jews but to people everywhere. This angered many Jews. Jesus seemed to be claiming that he was the son of God, able to forgive sins, and to them this was blasphemy.

By now Jesus realized he could not convince the Jewish people of the truth of his teachings. The Romans who ruled the Jews were also against him fearing that he would cause trouble. He felt that only by his death could he make his message clear, that the greatest thing in the world was love, and that those who believed in him would be reunited with God. He said, "Greater love hath no man than this, that a man lay down his life for his friends."

Jesus gathered with his disciples, to eat the simple Passover meal. He gave them a symbol by which they would remember him always. The Gospel tells us that he took bread and gave it to them, saying, "take, eat; this is my body." And he gave them wine saying, "This is my blood of the new testament, which is shed for many." On this simple ceremony is based the sacrament of the Lord's Supper which has ever since been one of the most important observances of Christianity, known today as Holy Communion, the Eucharist or the Mass.

Shortly after this Jesus was arrested and brought before the high priest and his council, who found him guilty of blasphemy punishable by death. They brought him before the Roman governor, Pilate, accusing him of calling himself King of the Jews. Pilate did not want trouble, and when he heard crowds shouting "Crucify him! Crucify him!" he condemned Jesus to death, and one more was added to the thousands whom the Romans executed by crucifixion.

All day Jesus hung upon the cross. As evening came he cried out, "My God, My God, why did you abandon me?" When darkness fell he said, "Father, in your hands I place my spirit," and died. The priests and rulers had killed his body, but had ensured that his spirit would live on in the minds of men.

*Jesus and his disciples at the "Last Supper"*

12

Jesus's body was placed in a tomb which was sealed and guarded. Two days later some of his followers came to the tomb and according to the Gospels, found his body gone. They recalled how Jesus had told them that he would rise from the dead, and were convinced that this had happened. They believed that ten days later he came before them, saying, "I have been given all authority in heaven and on earth. Go, then, to all peoples everywhere and make them my disciples: baptize them in the name of the Father, the Son and the Holy Spirit, and teach them to obey everything I have commanded you. And I will be with you always."

From then on, a wonderful faith filled them, and they faced ridicule, persecution and death to spread their gospel, that God loved all people, that Jesus had conquered death, and that belief in Jesus would bring happiness and everlasting life in heaven. These early messengers of Jesus were called apostles.

*The Crucifixion of Jesus*

# 5  The First Christian Church

Jesus, his disciples and their first converts, were Jews. They began to call themselves Christians, followers of Jesus Christ, but as Jews, they continued to keep Jewish laws and customs. When Christians worshipped Jesus as the Son of God and welcomed non-Jews, many were offended, and began to persecute the Christians.

A man named Saul was one of the persecutors until one day he was struck blind. He thought he heard a voice saying, "Saul, Saul, why do you persecute me?" Saul believed that Jesus was speaking to him. He became a Christian and was soon a leader among them. He changed his name to Paul, and travelled through the Roman

*A temple at Ephesus, one of the cities where Paul preached*

Empire, organizing Christian groups. He preached that three things were of overwhelming importance, faith, hope and above all love. Soon the disciple Peter became a missionary to Gentiles as well as to Jews.

Most people in the empire were poor, enslaved and unhappy. Many religions had spread among them but the people wanted one which gave them comfort and hope. Christianity provided this for it promised its believers a happy life in heaven after death. So Christianity grew.

In Rome men and women might be seen at night, stealing out of their houses, hurrying to some lonely spot on the city outskirts. They would enter a dark cave passing through dim passages, piled with coffins, to a big underground room. In these ancient catacombs where the Romans buried their dead, the Christians worshipped in secret, and here the religion which was to spread over most of the civilized world, slowly grew in strength and numbers.

To be a Christian then was not easy. They refused to worship the emperor, or fight in his armies. For many years they were persecuted but in spite of torture and death the religion spread — it seemed the only thing worth living and dying for. The sight of men and women bravely facing pain and death made others think its teachings must be true.

---

*Paul preaching the message of Jesus in Greece*

## The meaning of Christianity

What were their beliefs? The first century Christians thought of Jesus as the human side of a super-human spiritual God. His disciples felt that through Jesus they knew three sides of God: the powerful, loving Father, the personal human spirit in Jesus, and the impersonal spirit of God which entered into those who believed in him. So the idea of the Trinity (group of three) grew up: God the Father, God the Son and God the Holy Spirit.

At that time Christians believed in hell and its terrible punishments. In the fifth century Bishop Augustine wrote a book which greatly influenced Christians. It taught that mankind has inherited the sin of Adam and Eve when they ate the forbidden fruit in the Garden of Eden. All would be punished in hell unless God chose them to go to heaven.

Christians had increased so much in numbers by the early fourth century that the Roman Emperor Constantine decided to become Christian himself. He adopted the symbol of the cross and made Christianity the official religion of the Roman Empire. Christians now worshipped openly, in halls of justice or pagan temples, and soon began building special places of worship called churches.

Later the empire was divided in two. The eastern Roman Empire was centred on Constantinople, and the western Empire on Rome. As time passed, arguments grew between the East and West, and they grew apart, the western Church with services in Latin became known as the Catholic Church, and the eastern Church with Greek as the official language, was called the Orthodox Church.

*An Italian painting depicting the Eucharist, the ritual by which Christians believe they become part of Christ*

# 6  The Power of the Church

When Christianity became the official religion of the Roman empire, it was no longer the religion of the poor and persecuted, but of the rich and powerful. Its leaders did not live like Jesus and his disciples who had dwelled among the poor without home or possessions, but like princes. The Bishop of Rome, who was called the Pope, lived in a great palace controlling kings and emperors.

During the fourth, fifth and sixth centuries, the Roman Empire was overrun by barbarians. They admired and copied Roman life and customs and kept the Roman form of Christianity.

In A.D. 451, Attila and his Huns, from Asia, invaded Italy. His scouts reported the approach of an army. Attila had never before seen an army like this. A man dressed in white with a long white beard approached, leading men in golden robes, all singing. Attila and the man in white faced each other. "Who are you?" called Attila. "Leo," came the answer. It was the Pope, head of the Christian Church. Attila rode up to talk to the Pope; no-one knows what was said, but he turned and marched his army away from Rome, never to return.

The influence of the Christians grew. Popes dreamt of a world-wide church, ruling all nations and bringing peace to the world. It was a wonderful idea, but in trying to bring it about, they wanted to make all men think alike. This led to centuries of religious persecution. Meanwhile barbarian armies destroyed what had been civilized Roman provinces. The peasants were reduced to slavery; roads, cities, laws, cleanliness and all the advantages of Roman rule were gone. The light of civilization paled and grew dim.

*Pope Gregory VII, a great pope of the eleventh century*

# 7  Monasteries

While Church leaders gained power in Rome and Constantinople, and much of Europe was relapsing into barbarism, other Christians kept alive the simple message of Jesus, and the waning light of civilization. These were the monks, who felt that true service to God

*A monk illustrating a manuscript*

*A hermit's cell*

De la cause de leuure emprinse.
Premier chapitre.

Our ce que la multi
tude des liures et la
brieuete du temps et
la foiblesse du mémoire
ne seuffrent pas ses
choses qui sont escriptes estre com
prinses ensemble en vng courtage
ce mest aduis a moy qui suis le

moindre de tous mes freres en sacie.
Et ce puis ie scauoir en moy mesmes
qui ay veu leu et retourne plusieurs
liures y moult long temps assiduele
ment et curieusement. Et neatmoins
par le conseil dauscate de mes pl sou
uerains et greigneurs aulcuns ste
que iay esleues y mon petit engin
bien pou de tous ses liures de nře
foy catholique ou des liures payens

need not involve power, rich clothing and elaborate ceremonial.

They first lived as hermits, spending their time praying. Some never washed, letting lice, which they called the "pearls of God", increase on them; they considered this a sign of saintliness.

Men and women of exceptional goodness and holiness, were officially recognised by the Christian Church, and named saints. The disciples and apostles were so named, and many other Christian men and women who followed in the years to come.

In the sixth century a young Italian called Benedict, gave up his luxurious life and founded monasteries where groups of men called monks lived very simply, praying and working to produce their own food. They helped the poor, looked after the sick and gave hospitality to travellers.

Some monasteries established schools, but most restricted their education to the clergy. Pope Gregory wrote about this time, that learning other than the scriptures should be avoided, and the Church discouraged pagan learning.

With the founding of the monasteries came a revival in learning and culture. Monks read and copied ancient manuscripts, and studied science. Many were great scholars. Some developed agricultural and farming methods.

During the next four centuries more monasteries and new orders of monks were founded. They criticized the older monasteries for being too fond of wealth and leisure.

Most of the culture of ancient Rome was lost, but what little was saved was due to the monasteries which played a large part in reviving and spreading Christian art, architecture, music and letters, and kept alive the new ideas about farming and agriculture.

Later came friars, who insisted on complete poverty, earning their living working with the poor. St Francis of Assisi left a luxurious home and wandered as a barefooted friar, helping the poor and sick, and preaching of the happiness of a simple life. His followers, Little Brothers, were content to take what food and shelter the poor could offer. St Dominic left his Spanish university and founded the Black Friars who helped the poor and tried to convert people to Christianity.

These monks and friars kept the light of Christian civilization burning; besides prayers and toil, they developed church music, copied manuscripts, wrote books on theology and built beautiful abbeys.

---

*A twentieth-century Franciscan monk in Assisi, the birthplace of St Francis*

# 8 Crusades

Christians were often threatened by outside forces. In the seventh century in Arabia, the prophet Mohammed began preaching the new religion of Islam. Religious enthusiasm welded the scattered tribes into an Arab nation. Known as Moslems, they determined to spread the news of their faith, and believed that if killed fighting for their religion, they would go to heaven.

Syria, Persia, Egypt and the whole of North Africa were quickly overrun and included in an Arab Moslem empire. In A.D. 711 Moslems crossed into Spain, defeated the Christians and pressed on into France. In A.D. 732 they were overthrown by Charles Martel at the Battle of Tours, one of the most decisive battles in the history of the world. The Moslem threat to Christianity in the West was broken. In the East, Constantinople continued to resist for another 700 years.

In the eleventh century Moslem Turks captured Jerusalem and harassed the Christian pilgrims there. Constantinople was endangered and the Emperor appealed to Rome for help. The Pope called for a Crusade, a Holy War against the Moslem Turks.

With wild enthusiasm, rich and poor, old and young, left everything and started off for Palestine, known to Christians as the Holy Land.

Workmen threw down their hammers, left their workshops and took the nearest road to the East. They had no idea how far it was, or of how to get there, but they wanted to support the Pope in driving the

Moslems out of Jerusalem.

Princes and knights and their followers, ready to risk their lives for their religion and gain glory in battle, organised armies for the First Crusade. In 1099 they captured Jerusalem, but followed their victory by massacring thousands of Moslems and Jews. The crusaders came to their Holy City, praying to their God of Love who had given them this bloody victory.

A Christian kingdom was set up in Jerusalem, but the Moslems attacked again. The armies melted away and in 1187 Jerusalem was again under Moslem rule.

The Third Crusade in which the English King Richard I took part, failed to recover Jerusalem but

*Christians fight Moslems in the Third Crusade*

*Battling for the conquest of Jerusalem*

---

Saladin, the Moslem leader, agreed to let Christian pilgrims travel to the holy places.

Crusades continued: Constantinople was sacked by Christian crusaders, who tore the cathedral altar to pieces and a Latin kingdom was briefly set up in this centre of Greek Christianity. In 1212 there was even a Children's Crusade, and thousands of children set off to recover Jerusalem. Surely, they thought, God would deliver the city into the hands of innocent children. But this failed too, and the children were sold by Christian merchants to the Moslems.

Christian Palestine again fell to the Moslems. The results of the crusades were the final split of Christianity into East and West, the extended power and territory of the Moslems, and increased enmity between Christianity and Islam.

# 9  The Inquisition

Christians, like Jews, believed they had the only true religion. They accepted that God originally chose the Jews but believed that His favour had passed to Christians since the Jews had rejected Jesus.

A fundamental belief of the early Church was that God and Satan were competing for everyone's souls, and only through believing in Jesus and accepting Christian sacraments could human souls be saved from hell. Many Christians sincerely believed it was their duty to save non-Christians from this fate, even if it meant forcing Christianity upon them by war or torture. They thought all other religions were false, and missionaries were sent to convert the

*An English martyr being burnt at the stake by the Inquisition*

misguided heathen peoples outside Christendom.

Church leaders were just as intolerant of Christians who dared to question the beliefs of the official Church. They were labelled heretics.

The main aim of St Dominic's Black Friars was to convert people to Christianity, and to root out heresy. Pope Innocent III ordered the rulers of the Catholic countries to help the Black Friars in their task. An investigation called the Holy Inquisition was set up, to "redeem those Christians who had strayed from the true faith". The Inquisition became a way of terrorising anyone who criticised the Church or its leaders, by torture, and death by burning. The Black Friars searched out heretics and brought them to trial. There was no court of appeal, and those found guilty were fined, imprisoned, tortured, or burned at the stake.

As criticism of the Church continued, more and more victims of the Inquisition suffered torture and death, but in spite of this, or perhaps because of it, their ideas spread.

In England, John Wycliffe translated the Bible into English. He had powerful friends who saved him from death but some of his followers did not escape. John Huss in Bohemia was influenced by Wycliffe and spoke against the priests. He too was burned at the stake. These and many other brave men who suffered death rather than renounce their beliefs, are known as martyrs.

---

*John Huss of Bohemia being interrogated by the Council of the Church*

# 10   The Orthodox Church

The eastern Orthodox Church and the western Roman Church were very similar. The division between them was political rather than religious. In the East each city had a leading priest known as the Patriarch but the Emperor in Constantinople maintained control. The government used the Church to keep and extend its power.

When Rome was little more than a ruin, Constantinople was still a mighty city and centre of an empire. The eastern Church spread Christianity to the slav countries of Bulgaria, Serbia and Russia. But after the fall of Constantinople to the Moslems in 1453 only the Russians remained free. Moscow became the centre of what was by then called Orthodox Christianity and the Christian Church became largely the servant of the government.

The beliefs and ceremonies of the Orthodox Church remained similar to the Catholic Church, but there was no one person with power like the Pope. Many saints

*Theodora, Empress to Justinian I of Constantinople, a great emperor of the eastern Empire*

are honoured in the Orthodox Church and beautiful portraits called icons are displayed in church and home.

At baptism the child is immersed three times in water. Confirmation follows soon after when the forehead and other parts of the body are anointed. In the marriage ceremony bride and groom are crowned with crowns or garlands. They share a cup of wine symbolizing the sharing in marriage, and walk in a circle to show, like the circle, that their marriage has no end. Divorce is rarely allowed, but if agreed, the Orthodox Church will bless a divorced person wishing to remarry. Lighted candles are held at funerals symbolizing that the spirit of the departed person is not extinguished.

## Worship in a Greek Orthodox Church

# 11    The Catholic Church

The Roman Church claims to be the true interpreter of the teachings of Jesus, and to have inherited the authority which he gave to Peter when he said "Thou art Peter, and on this rock I will build my church." Catholics are therefore guided by the tradition of the earliest Church.

Today the beliefs and practices of the Roman Catholic Church are nearer to those of the thirteenth or the fourth century than almost any other Christian group, and the Catholic Church has more members than all other Christian Churches combined.

Catholics accept that the Pope is God's representative on earth and that on matters of supreme importance he is guided by God and his decisions are binding. Catholic means universal and as they believe Jesus desired complete unity for his Church, all good Catholics try to obey the Pope's wishes.

Catholics believe all people are born in sin and they must atone (make amends) for this. Suffering may be part of this atonement and may therefore be good. The Resurrection of Jesus promises life after death, either happily in heaven, or terrifyingly in hell. By their own free will Catholics choose heaven or hell.

They believe that love, the basis of Christianity, is possible only through grace which is a gift of

*The Virgin Mary with Jesus and two saints, to whom Catholics pray in addition to the Trinity*

God. Grace is given through the sacraments. Baptism or Christening, is being received into Christ's Church. The priest pours water on the head symbolizing the washing away of sin. Catholics consider Baptism so important that it must be carried out soon after birth. They believe that if a baby dies unbaptized, it will not receive the full happiness of Heaven although God provides a state of happiness called Limbo for them. The sacrament of Con-

*A mother and child praying in a Catholic church in London*

firmation is given when a person is old enough to understand the meaning of being a baptized Christian, when a bishop anoints the forehead with holy oil in the form of a cross.

The Blessed Eucharist celebrates the Last Supper. Catholics believe that a miracle took place

when Jesus celebrated the Last Supper and that the bread and wine became part of his body, and he was actually united with his disciples. They believe that the power to repeat this miracle was given to the apostles who passed it on to their successors, the bishops and priests. They consecrate bread and wine, and by the miracle called Transubstantiation, turn it into the actual body of Jesus, giving it to believers to eat and drink in the ceremony of the Mass. This is called receiving Communion.

Catholics who commit sin must receive the sacrament of Penance before receiving communion. They confess the sin to a priest who asks them for an Act of Contrition, asking forgiveness from God. If they commit a serious sin, called Mortal sin, they must receive Absolution, before receiving God's grace. Extreme Unction is the sac-

*The sacrament of Orders — men being ordained as priests in the Catholic Church*

rament given to the dying.

The sacrament of marriage is a binding agreement to live faithfully together, and to bring up their children as Catholics. Divorce is not allowed by the Catholic Church although sometimes the Pope will permit a separation. The sacrament of Orders makes a man a member of the Priesthood.

Catholics pray to God the Father, the Son and the Holy Spirit (the Trinity), and also to the saints, especially the Virgin Mary, mother of Jesus.

# 12 Reformation

Some critics of the Catholic Church were so disillusioned that they believed the only remedy was to break away and found new Christian churches. In 1510 a German monk named Martin Luther, went to Rome and was horrified to see the Italian priests "making sport of true religion". He found that Indulgences were being sold promising forgiveness of sins.

*The German monk Martin Luther, teaching the story of the gospels to children*

## Revolt against Rome

Luther returned to Germany, wrote out how he thought the Church should be reformed to bring back its former true Christianity, and nailed this on the church door at Wittenberg. He was declared a heretic by the Pope. Following Luther's action a Church was formed with simple forms of worship, using services and scriptures in language which all could understand without the aid of priests. Lutheran churches were established in Germany, and also in Scandinavia.

In England it suited the policies of King Henry VIII to break the connection between the English churches and Rome. An Act of Parliament made the King head of the Anglican Church. The new Church became as intolerant as the Catholic Church and all English people had to attend their Anglican place of worship. Those still practising the Catholic religion suffered much persecution and worshipped in secret. The Anglican Church retained many Catholic beliefs and methods of organisation, including the power of bishops. But the Bible had been translated into English and people were for the first time able to read it in their own language and began thinking for themselves.

These changes in the Christian religion became known as the Reformation, and the 'reformers', or 'protesters' broke away from the Church of Rome and formed themselves into various Protestant churches.

*The first English translation of the Bible being presented to Henry VIII*

## Spread of Protestantism

In 1620 a group of English reformers sailed to North America. These reformers, called Puritans, felt the English Church was too much like the Roman Church. They were not allowed to worship as they wished. They went to America in order to have religious freedom. These were the 'Pilgrim Fathers' and they founded Puritan churches there. Other Protestant groups from Holland and Germany followed, colonising and setting up churches.

Attempts to establish Protestant churches in western Europe sometimes brought about civil war, and were followed by increased activity by the Inquisition. In France John Calvin preached Protestant ideas, but was forced to escape to Switzerland, where he established a Calvinist Church. In France his followers were called Huguenots. Only after centuries of persecution and civil war were they allowed to worship as they wished. Some were expelled from France, and fled to England. John Knox took Calvin's ideas to Scotland, where his followers were known as Presbyterians.

The Protestants divided into many sects, each emphasizing certain aspects of Christianity. Although their beliefs and forms of worship differed from one another, there was one fundamental difference between all Protestants and the Catholic and Orthodox Churches; they considered only two sacraments essential; Baptism, and Holy Communion. Protestants believed the bread and wine were symbols and did not become the actual body and blood of Jesus.

*John Calvin preaching in France before his banishment to Switzerland*

## Counter-Reformation

Catholic leaders realized that they must find some answer to the Protestants, and in 1545 a Great Council of the Church was called at Trent. The conduct of priests and bishops improved but beliefs and teachings were unchanged.

In 1534, Ignatius Loyola, a Spanish soldier, formed the Society of Jesus or Jesuits. They considered themselves soldiers of Christ, and devoted their lives to spreading Catholic Christianity. Some taught children to be loyal to the Catholic Church. Others went as missionaries wherever the Pope might send them.

The Catholic leaders at Trent would not compromise with the Protestants and the Inquisition became more active and merciless than ever.

The Roman Church was now known as the Roman Catholic Church, and it retained its hold on much of southern and western Europe.

*The Council of the Catholic Church, meeting at Trent*

# 13  Protestant Beliefs

After the Reformation Protestants divided into many groups, each emphasizing certain aspects of Christianity. The Congregationalists had no bishops; the congregation of each church (or chapel) being self-governing. Others formed the Baptists who placed great stress on baptism (immersion in water to wash away sin). Many Baptists emigrated to America, and are now a strong denomination in the United States. Another group, Unitarians, did not accept the Trinity, but worshipped only one absolute God.

The Society of Friends, or Quakers, was formed in 1650. They believed that each person shares God's grace, so had no priests and any member could address the group if God's spirit so moved him. They have always believed the simple commandment ''Thou shalt not kill,'' means exactly that, and refuse to take part in anything connected with taking life. They were fiercely persecuted by other Protestant groups, but are now much respected for the simplicity of their religion.

During the eighteenth century many Anglican clergy became lax in their duties, spending their time in fox-hunting and other pleasures, and ignoring the working people who lived in great poverty. John Wesley, an Anglican clergyman, devoted his life to preaching and working with the poor, travelling about the countryside. Many Anglican churches were closed to him so he preached in churchyards and market places. His many followers called Methodists, established

*Holy Communion at an Anglican church*

39

*A Methodist service on a veranda in Sarawak*

churches in Britain and America. Methodists now form a large Protestant force in the world.

In the United States the Jehovah's Witness movement arose in the nineteenth century. They worshipped Jehovah as the one and only true God. In 1830 Joseph Smith formed the Mormon Church, whose headquarters are now in Utah. Their beliefs are based on the Bible and on the Book of Mormon.

In 1860 an Englishman William Booth, felt the Anglican Church was failing to reach many of the people

*A member of the Congregationalist Church in Africa*

*Jehovah's Witnesses being baptized*

who most needed help, and he began preaching to down-and-outs, drunkards and others. He adopted the title of The Salvation Army. Their message was simple: the reality of sin and its consequences, but with Jesus's promise of forgiveness. With its emphasis on help to the needy, the Salvation Army provides a valued service in modern life.

There are many other Protestant sects throughout the world, each with their own beliefs and forms of worship. Most Protestants permit divorce but some will not allow divorced people to remarry in church.

# 14 Christian Festivals

Christian festivals are closely connected with the life of Jesus. The first main holy day (holiday) is the day of his birth, celebrated on December 25th by Catholics and Protestants, and on January 9th by the Orthodox Church. It is not certain when Jesus was born. Christmas almost certainly grew from pagan festivals, celebrating the

*Children dressed as angels sing Christmas carols*

passing of the old and birth of the new year, and this date would have more easily persuaded pagans to become Christian.

Christians rejoice and thank God for the gift of His Son at Christmas and celebrate by giving presents, or Christmas boxes, often

*These sculptures commemorate Jesus's last steps to his Crucifixion, a journey which is retraced by worshippers every Easter*

*A Spanish religious brotherhood, the Hermandades, in procession during Holy Week*

on the following day called Boxing Day.

Easter, celebrated in Spring, is the festival for the Crucifixion of Jesus; and his resurrection, which

Jerusalem. It used to be a period of fasting and many Christians still observe this custom. Ash Wednesday is the first day of Lent and is preceded by Shrove Tuesday when Christians were shriven (their sins forgiven). Many Catholic countries celebrate a festival called Carnival during the days before Lent. Palm Sunday at the end of Lent begins Holy Week, commemorating the day when Jesus entered Jerusalem with his disciples. Maundy Thursday commemorates the Last Supper. Good Friday is a day of mourning for the Crucifixion when Christians worship in silent bare churches, but on Easter Sunday all is bright with flowers, lights and music. Christians rejoice in the belief of the resurrection and divinity of Jesus, and promise of eternal life.

The name Easter is thought to come from Eostre, the Anglo-Saxon god of spring and gifts of easter eggs may symbolize the new life given by Jesus when he rose from the dead.

Ascension is celebrated forty days after Easter, commemorating Jesus being taken into heaven, and ten days later is Pentecost, when the apostles received the gift of the Holy Spirit and the Christian Church was born. Pentecost used to be favoured for baptism, and as white was worn for this, it came to be called Whit Sunday.

is the fundamental belief of Christianity.

The forty days of Lent commemorate the time Jesus spent in the wilderness before entering

# 15  Missionaries

Europeans were great explorers, and usually one object of exploration was to spread Christianity.

In 1518 the Spaniard Cortes led an expedition to the unknown land of Mexico in quest for gold, and war against heathens in the name of Christianity. They reached Mexico City, rich capital of the Aztec empire, where their religious zeal overcame their greed for gold and they interfered with the Aztec temples, and tried to convert the people to Christianity. Thousands of angry Aztecs rose against them, killing many, but Cortes returned.

*Jesuit priests preaching to a tribe of Indians*

Eventually Mexico was ruled by Spain, and Catholic cathedrals replaced Aztec temples.

In South America too, Catholic missionaries pushed far into the interior, converting the natives and founding churches. Most people in South America today are Catholics. In the seventeenth century French fur traders opened up forest streams in Canada, and often ahead

*An Anglican missionary in nineteenth-century Africa*

of them Jesuit priests pressed on into unknown country, founding Catholic communities.

The Catholic Portuguese were great explorers. They sailed around the African coast taking missionaries who converted a few tribal chiefs and founded Catholic missions. In North Africa most people were Moslems and they hated Christian Europeans, remembering the Crusades. Further south Christians were also hated because the main reason for their presence had been to obtain slaves.

In the nineteenth century missionary activity greatly increased. Rivalry between various Protestant Churches, and between Catholics and Protestants, led to an increase in missionaries all anxious to make converts to their own brand of Christianity. They pressed on into unexplored country, opened schools and gave medical help to the natives, and brought to light the horrors of the African slave trade.

Missionaries travelled all over the world, founding churches, opening schools and medical centres in India, China and other parts of the far East. They brought Christian ideas to many of the natives.

*Boys in an African Methodist school today*

# 16   Christianity and Science

The Christian Church was not noted for its interest in science. No scientific explanation of the universe was possible when Christianity was developing, and early religious thinkers believed the wonders around them were caused by God's actions.

The stories told to explain the universe were believed by all Christians and were never questioned. The Jewish idea of a jealous God was accepted by Christian leaders. Christians also agreed with Jews that Man was the centre of the Universe and reason for all creation.

*Galileo demonstrating how the earth moves round the sun*

## Science in the Middle Ages

In 1543 a Pole named Copernicus suggested that the sun, not the earth, was the centre of the universe, and that the earth went round it. Church leaders at first explained his theory as merely a useful idea to simplify astronomical calculations. They said a mathematician's idea could not affect God's truth.

Bruno, an Italian monk thought otherwise, and taught that

*Charles Darwin, scientist and author*

the theory of Copernicus was correct. He was persecuted in Rome and fled to Switzerland, but the Calvinists too would have nothing to do with such irreligious nonsense. So he went to England. His ideas were not welcomed there and he returned to Italy and in 1600 was burned at the stake as a heretic.

Later the invention of the telescope proved that the earth really did go round the sun. The Italian Galileo, stated his agreement with the theory of Copernicus and was called to Rome, where he had to promise not to express these views. Later he wrote a book, again stating his ideas. He was called before the Inquisition and forced to deny the truth of his belief that the earth moves round the sun. It is said that he muttered under his breath, "But it does move." It was a long time before the true facts about the sun, earth and planets were accepted by the Christian Church.

## Charles Darwin

A bigger shock came in 1859 when Darwin published his book *The Origin of Species*, arguing that Man was not a special creation of God, but the result of an age-long process of evolution from animal ancestors. This was more revolutionary than the idea of Copernicus, for it made Man himself the result of accidental forces.

The book appeared when thinking people were questioning Christian dogma. Some Christians were worried about many traditional beliefs, but Church leaders would not tolerate such free-thinking, which they felt endangered Church and state. In 1853 people in Britain, including a university professor and a railway workman, were dismissed from their jobs because they did not believe in hell. There are people today who believe every sentence in the Bible was dictated by God and must therefore mean exactly what it says.

Scientific findings stimulated atheists and critics of religion against whom the Church was fighting a losing battle. Many Christians nowadays accept the fact of evolution, but believe the truth of their religion is not necessarily affected by it.

*Nicholas Copernicus*

# 17  Changing Christianity

The twentieth century has seen Christian attitudes change in many directions: towards science, other religions, chastity, contraception, divorce and Christian unity.

Christian influence has declined in many parts of the world. Old beliefs have faded. Loyalty to the Pope and belief in the Catholic Church has weakened. Many Protestants no longer attend church.

Christians often failed to see that in many ways the other great religions agreed with their ideas. They wanted the whole world to accept their doctrines, fearing that other religions threatened their Faith. Until recently there had been little co-operation between different religions, or between the numerous Christian sects. Christianity like other faiths, stressed that it alone had the truth. Even with Islam and Judaism, which worshipped the same God, there was no common ground because of the fundamental Christian belief in the divinity of Jesus, which is not shared by Moslems or Jews. Most Christians believe that the divinity of Christ is the essential part of Christianity. The enmity of the crusades has gone but unity is still far away.

Christian treatment of Jews has been very bad; Jews have been reviled and persecuted for their part in bringing about the death of Jesus, 2000 years ago. But this is changing, and in 1959 Pope John removed the phrase accusing the Jews from Good Friday services.

## Christianity and Communism

Revolutionary governments see religion as an obstacle to their rule. Communists have called religion the opium of the people, meaning a drug which makes them unthinkingly subservient to their rulers. When the Communists came to power in Russia, they declared that God did not exist. Bishops and priests were murdered and monasteries closed down. The Patriarch of the Orthodox Church was imprisoned and thousands of priests and church members who refused to renounce their belief were sent to concentration camps. But after twenty years of repression, it was found that nearly half the population were still Christians.

In Poland, a Communist country, about eighty per cent of the population are church-going Roman Catholics. In 1978, for the first time a Polish Cardinal was chosen as Pope, John Paul II.

## Christianity as a state religion

Since the days of Constantine, the Christian Church has preferred to defend the state rather than change it to produce a more Christ-like society. Many people attracted to Christianity by the love and care for the unfortunate shown by Jesus, joined socialist or communist groups, which seemed hostile to the Church.

In most Christian countries rulers have used the Christian Church to obtain obedience from their subjects. Leading churchmen have been given important positions and it was in their interest to support the governing class. In Britain until the mid-nineteenth century no man could hold public office or teach in universities unless he belonged to the Church of England.

In Catholic countries like Italy and Southern Ireland, laws on birth control, abortion and divorce are based upon Catholic religious ideas. There is opposition to this religious control over what many people think are matters of individual conscience. In Protestant countries some Christians fear sexual freedom has increased too much and would like to use the old laws to force their ideas upon everyone, as the Church used to do.

*Catholics in Communist Poland*

*far left*
*A modern look to the Anglican church of St Martin-in-the-Fields*

## Christianity in South America

About 300 million of the world's 700 million Catholics live in South America. Most of the governments there are very repressive and the people live in great poverty. In January 1979 a conference of South American Catholics was opened by the Pope, who has to give the lead in deciding what policy is right for the Catholic Church. The extent to which religion should be engaged in politics, if at all, is a question facing many Christians today, and the Church is deeply divided on this.

*Pope John Paul II*

54

# 18    Christianity Today

The simple story of the Gospels, and the emphasis Jesus placed on love and forgiveness, have always inspired Christians and ensured that Christianity has continued to grow and to renew its spirit. Nowadays most Christian groups live peaceably together and co-operate in trying to solve the world's problems.

The World Council of Churches was formed in 1948. They take action on many problems of the modern world and give aid to peoples fighting to gain their freedom by speaking and acting against oppressive governments. Everywhere Christian Churches are doing much to help the poor and oppressed, but many Christians feel that much more could be done

*Celebrating the dedication of a Methodist church in West Africa*

*A Christian child lights a candle in church to represent her prayers*

The Catholic Church has recently moved towards Christian unity and in 1958 Pope John XXIII narrowed the gulf between Catholic and Protestant Churches. His suc-

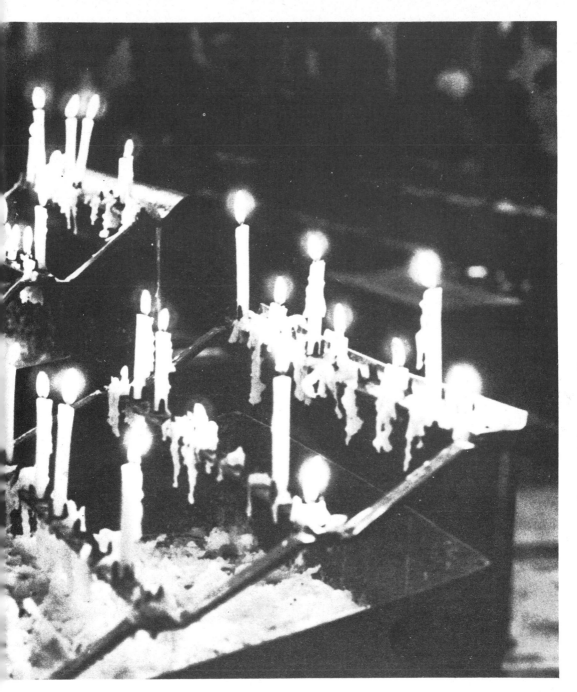

cessor Pope Paul VI met the head of the Orthodox Church in Jerusalem in 1964, the first meeting between Pope and Patriarch for 500 years. In 1965 he addressed the United Nations Assembly in New York, appealing for universal peace. In 1978 the Archbishop of Canterbury, head of the Anglican Church, joined the celebrations at the election of a new Pope in Rome, the first such visit for over 400 years.

A Christian might therefore feel that Christian Churches are nearer now to the teachings of Jesus than they have often been in the past. He might justify his faith in Christianity by saying that it is universal, not restricted to one area or to one people, but with a message for everyone for it believes that all are equal before God. He believes in a personal loving God, guiding mankind to a better way of life and a life after death, and that God's love was shown by the life of Jesus. Christians therefore try always to recognize the dignity, and respect the freedom of others and ensure that all their actions are based on love.

Some Christians are not sure they can accept all the doctrines of the Christian Church but are convinced that the life, teaching and example of Jesus give us the best guide for human behaviour.

*Children in a convent in the east end of London*

# Glossary

**Apostle** Messenger who preached the gospel of Jesus, particularly the twelve disciples.

**Baptism** The ceremony of name-giving, when a person is received into the Christian Church by the sprinkling with or immersion in water, by the priest or minister.

**Barbarians** People from outside the Roman Empire, non-Christian and often wild and uncivilized.

**Blasphemy** To speak against God.

**Catacombs** Underground cemeteries where the Romans used to bury their dead.

**Confirmation** The sacrament given to a baptized Christian at an age when he or she can understand its meaning.

**Congregation** People gathered together, especially in a church.

**Crusades** Military expeditions organised by the Pope, when Christians tried to win back the Holy Land from the Moslems.

**Eucharist** The sacrament based on the Lord's Supper, when Jesus and his disciples celebrated the Passover before he was arrested. Also known as Holy Communion and the Mass.

**Gospel** The good news or message of Jesus as told by Matthew, Mark, Luke and John.

**Heretic** Someone who did not agree with the doctrines of the Christian faith practised in his own country.

**Hermit** An early Christian who chose to live alone, often in a cave, eating very little and spending much time in prayer.

**Indulgences** Privileges granted by pope or bishop, which remitted the punishment due for a committed sin.

**Inquisition** A Roman Catholic court for searching out and punishing heretics.

**Islam** An arabic word meaning 'submission' which is the name for the Moslem religion.

**Martyr** Someone who suffers hardship or is put to death because he will not renounce his religious beliefs.

**Messiah** The saviour who the Jews hoped God would send to deliver them from their sufferings, and bring about a world of peace.

**Missionary** Someone who under-takes to spread the Christian relig-ion among non-believers.

**Passover** The Jewish feast held every year in memory of their escape from slavery in Egypt.

**Patriarch** A leading bishop of the Orthodox Church.

**Persecution** Causing harassment and suffering to people because they have different opinions or beliefs.

**Puritans** People who disagreed with the Anglican religion. Many of them went to America where they hoped to find more religious free-dom.

**Resurrection** The arising of Jesus from the dead.

**Sacrament** A religious ceremony regarded as the outward sign of spiritual grace.

**Transubstantiation** The miracul-ous change of the bread and wine of the Last Supper into the body and blood of Jesus Christ.

**Trinity** Union of three — God the Father, God the Son and God the Holy Ghost.

# More Books

*Bible Stories,* by David Kossoff (Collins).
*Good News Bible.* The Bible Societies (Collins/Fontana).
*Religions of Mankind,* by Canon H.K.Luce (Christophers).
*The History of World Religions,* by Katherine Savage (Bodley Head).
*The Holy Bible,* King James Version (Collins).
*The Orthodox Church,* by Sergei Hackel (Ward Lock).
*World Faiths,* by Liva Baker (Abelard-Schuman).

# Index

# Picture acknowledgements

The author and publishers wish to thank all those who have given permission for copyright pictures to be reproduced on the following pages: Catholic Herald, 42, 54, 56-7, 58; Methodist Missionary Society, 7, 40 (upper), 48, 55; Italian State Tourist Office, 14, 31; Radio Times Hulton Picture Library, 6, 11, 30, 32, 33, 38-9, 40 (lower), 41, 43, 44-5, 53; Pat Hodgson, 10, 15, 16, 19, 34, 36, 37, 46, 52; Mansell Collection, 8, 9, 13, 18.